THE
PHILOSOPHY
OF BEARDS

THOMAS S. GOWING

THE BRITISH LIBRARY

First published in 1854 by J. Haddock

This edition published in 2014 by
The British Library
96 Euston Road
London NW1 2DB

British Library Cataloguing in Publication Data
A catalogue record for this book is available from the British Library

ISBN 978 0 7123 5766 1

Designed and typeset in Monotype Bulmer
by illuminati, Grosmont
Printed in England by TJ International

CONTENTS

PREFACE

THE following Lecture, the first I believe on the specific subject, met with a warm reception from a numerous and good-humoured auditory; and received long and flattering notices from the local papers, the *Ipswich Journal*, and the *Suffolk Chronicle*. My enterprising and liberal publisher, has thought it worthy of more extended circulation. May the public think with him, and take it off his hands as freely as he has taken it off mine!

I have modified the passages which referred to the illustrations; the greater portion of which it would, independently of expense, have been impossible to give with any effect on a small scale. Mr. F.B. Russel, (to whom, with his worthy brother artist, Mr. Thomas Smyth, I was indebted for the original design) has, with a kindness I can better appreciate than acknowledge, anastaticized the humorous drawing of the ape and the goat, with which their joint talents enriched my Lecture.

Since its delivery, many notes have been added to the Lecture, which it is hoped will afford both amusement and information. It now only remains for me to make my bow, wish my *fratres barbati* long life to their Beards, and shout

Pivat Regina!
Floreat Barba!

INTRODUCTION

OUR most universal and most imaginative Poet, whose single lines are often abstracts and epitomes of poems, makes Hamlet exclaim—"What a piece of work is man! How noble in reason! how infinite in faculties! in form and moving, how express and admirable! in action, how like an angel! in apprehension, how like a God! the beauty of the world! the paragon of animals!" And yet this same glorious creature, thus worthily praised, is, with singular contradiction, so forgetful of his higher attributes, that he can despise his reason! ignore his infinite faculties! deliberately deface that form so express and admirable! descend to actions that smack rather of the demon than the angel! Drown his godlike apprehension in drink! Shave off his majestic beauty! and become, instead of the paragon—the parody of animals!

O Fashion! most mighty, but most capricious of goddesses! what strange vagaries playest thou with the sons and daughters of men! What is there so lovely, that thou canst not, with a word, transform into an object of disgust and abhorrence? What so ugly and repulsive, but thou hast the art to exalt it into a golden image for thy slaves to worship, on pain of the fiery furnace of ridicule? Could a collection be made of the forms and figures, modes and mummeries, which thou hast imposed on thy ofttimes too willing votaries, it would task the most vivid imagination, the most fantastic stretch of fancy, to furnish a description of the incongruous contents!

Perhaps no human feature has been more the subject of Fashion's changeable humours than the BEARD, of which it is purposed to night to render some account, in the hope of being able to prove that in no instance has she been guilty of more deliberate offences against nature and reason! With this object in view, the structure, intention, and uses of the Beard will be examined, and its artistic relations indicated; its history will next be traced; and a reply will then be briefly given to some objections against wearing the Beard, not embraced in the preceding matter.

PHYSIOLOGY

A QUAINT old Latin author asks, "What is a Beard? Hair? and what is Hair? a Beard?" Perhaps a Beard may be defined more clearly by stating, that in its full extent it comprehends all hair visible on the countenance below the eyes, naturally growing down the sides of the face, crossing the cheeks by an inverted arch, fringing the upper and lower lips, covering the chin above and below, and hanging down in front of the neck and throat:—moustaches and whiskers being merely parts of a general whole. The hair of the head differs from that of the Beard. In an enlarged microscopical view, the former is seen to resemble a flattened cylinder, tapering off towards the extremity. It has a rough outer bark, and a finer inner coat; and contains, like a plant, its central pith, consisting of oil and coloring matters. At the lower part it is bulbous, and the pith vessels rest on a large vesicle. The bulb is enclosed in a fold of the skin, and imbedded in the sebaceous glands. The root is usually inserted obliquely to the surface. Avoiding further detail, let me at once direct your attention to the circumstance, that whereas the hair of the head is only furnished with one pith tube, that of the Beard, is provided with two.* Is not this a striking fact to commence with? and does it not at once suggest that this extra provision must have a special purpose? It has, as we shall presently see; and only

---

* Vide Hassell's Microscopic Anatomy. Haller says "Withof calculated that the hair of the Beard grows at the rate of 1½ line in the week, which is 6½ inches in the year, and by the time a man reaches eighty, 27 feet will have fallen under the edge of the razor."

now add, that the hairs of the Beard are more deeply inserted and more durable; flatter, and hence more disposed to curl.

As the Beard makes its appearance simultaneously with one of the most important natural changes in man's constitution, it has in all ages been regarded as the ensign of manliness. All the leading races of men, whether of warm or cold climates, who have stamped their character on history—Egyptians, Indians, Jews, Assyrians, Babylonians, Persians, Arabs, Greeks, Romans, Celts, Turks, Scandinavians, Sclaves—were furnished with an abundant growth of this natural covering. Their enterprizes were accordingly distinguished by a corresponding vigour and daring. The fact, too, is indisputable, that their hardiest efforts were contemporaneous with the existence of their Beards; and a closer investigation would show that the rise and fall of this natural feature has had more influence on the progress and decline of nations, than has hitherto been suspected. Though there are *individual* exceptions, the absence of Beard is usually a sign of physical and moral weakness; and in degenerate tribes wholly without, or very deficient, there is a conscious want of manly dignity, and contentedness with a low physical, moral, and intellectual condition. Such tribes have to be sought for by the physiologist and ethnologist; the *historian* is never called upon to do honor to their deeds. Nor is it without significance that the effeminate Chinese have signalized their present attempt to become once more free men, instead of tartar tools—by a formal resolve to have done with pigtails, and let their hair take its natural course over head and chin.*

---

* The whiskers of Confucius are said to be preserved as relics in China.

But the hair does not merely act as an external sign; it has, or it would not be there, its own proper and distinct functions to perform. The most important of these is the protection of some of the most susceptible portions of our frame from cold and moisture—those fruitful sources of painful, and often fatal, disease. And what more admirable contrivance could be thought of for this purpose than a free and graceful veil of hair—a substance possessing the important properties of power to repel moisture, and to serve as a non-conductor of heat and electricity.

Let me now show you what lies underneath the surface naturally covered by the Beard. We have first that ganglion or knot, the seat of the exquisitely painful affection *tic doloureux*. From it you will perceive white threads of nerves radiating to the jaws precisely in the line protected by the Beard. As you contemplate it, you can hardly fail to be struck with the fact, that in shaving may sometimes originate that local paralysis which disfigures the corners of the mouth. Next we have the nerves of the teeth, which all know to be so affected by changes of temperature.

Glance now, if you please, at those glands which secrete and elaborate the lymph which is to form part of the circulating fluid, and in which scrofula often has its origin, and some say its name. They are peculiarly liable to be affected by cold and moisture, presenting then those well-known unsightly swellings about the neck: they therefore receive an extra protection, the hair usually growing much more thickly on the parts where they are met with than elsewhere.

There is another set of glands, the sebaceous, which are thickly concentrated on the chin. Now shaving is the cause that the hairs on this part are liable to a peculiar and very irritating disease, which imparts a kind of foretaste of purgatory to many unfortunate victims of that unnatural practice. Those with strong beards most righteously suffer the most; for the more efficient the natural protection is, the greater is also the folly of its removal.

Lastly, there are the tonsils, and the glands of the throat and larynx. Few require to be told how common at present are acute and chronic affections of these parts.

That the Beard was intended as a protection to the whole of them, any one may satisfy himself by wearing it and then shaving it off in cold or damp weather. If not inclined to try this experiment, and mind I do not recommend it, perhaps the following evidence will be sufficiently convincing.

Firstly, the historical fact that the Russian soldiers, when compelled to shave by Peter the Great, suffered most severely.

Secondly, the medical testimony extracted from the *Professional Dictionary* of Dr. Copeland, one of the first Physicians of the day, where it is stated,

> Persons in the habit of wearing long Beards, have often been affected with rheumatic pains in the face, or with sore throat on shaving them off. In several cases of chronic sore throat, wearing the Beard under the chin, or upon the throat, has prevented a return of the complaint.

Thirdly, the fact that several persons in this town (Ipswich) have been so cured. And lastly, this brief but important testimony of the men of the Scottish Central Railway, dated Perth, 24th August, 1853.

We, the servants of the Scottish Central Railway, beg to inform you, that having last summer seen a circular recommending the men employed upon railways to cultivate the growth of their Beards, as the best protection against the inclemency of the weather, have been induced to follow this advice; and the benefit we have derived from it, induces us to recommend it to the general adoption of our brothers in similar circumstances throughout the kingdom. We can assure them, from our own experience, that they will by this means be saved from the bad colds and sore throats of such frequent occurrence without this natural protection.

Signed by 5 Guards, 1 Inspector of Police, 2 Engine Men, and 1 Fireman.

Let us next see, for it is a highly interesting point in a consumption-breeding climate like ours, where thousands of victims annually die, *how* the entrances to the air passages and lungs are protected by the upper part of the beard – the moustache. We draw air in commonly through the nose, and breathe it out through the mouth: though occasionally the two passages exchange functions. In a section of the nose, the interior of the nostril is seen to communicate, by a slightly curved passage, with the back entrance to the mouth and throat. Now as the incoming air must follow the direction of the draught, you will readily perceive that any air entering by the nostrils must pass through or over the hair of the moustache, and be warmed in the passage: and when the air makes its way by the mouth, it must pass under the moustache and be warmed, like that under the eaves of a thatched roof.

The moustache, however, not merely warms the inspired air, but filters it from superfluous moisture, dirt, dust, and smoke; and soon we trust it will be deemed as rational to deprive the upper lip of its protecting fringe, as to shave the eyebrows or pluck out the eyelashes.*

Those to whom the extent of preventible disease among our artizans—disease arising solely from their employments is unknown, I must refer to Mr. Thackrah's book on that specific subject. Scientific ingenuity had long attempted to devise contrivances to relieve the men from some of these diseases; but the schemes were found too cumbrous, or otherwise impracticable. As so often happens, what *men* were profoundly searching for, *nature* had placed directly under their noses. Mr. Chadwick, to whom the public are indebted for much valuable information on questions connected with the public health, and Dr. Alison, of Glasgow, one of whom had seen the particles of iron settling on and staining the Beards of foreign smiths; and the other had noticed the dusty Beards of foreign masons when at work, were led to the conclusion, independently of each other, that the iron and stone dust were much better deposited on the Beard (whence they could be washed), than in the lungs, where they would be sure to cause disease. The lungs of a mason for instance are preserved in Edinburgh, which are one concrete mass of stone. These gentlemen published their convictions; and through the beneficial agency of the press, that information, aided by papers in the *Builder*, and in *Dickens's Household Words*, soon found its way to our

---

* I can from personal experience state, that being subject when younger to swelling of the upper lip from cold, previous to entering Switzerland I allowed my moustache to grow. During six weeks excursion on foot, exposed to all weathers and stopping for none, being at one moment in warm valleys and a few hours afterwards at the top of ice-clad mountains, I never felt the least uncomfortableness about the mouth. When on returning home, however, I was foolish enough to shave, I paid dearly for the operation.

artizans, many of whom have tried the experiment, and borne testimony to its satisfactory results. At this juncture, let us also hope that the reiterated opinions of eminent Army Surgeons will at length be listened to, and the British Soldier be freed from the apoplectic leathern stock, and allowed to wear that protection which nature endowed him with. To the latter the most rigid economist cannot object, since it will add nothing to the estimates, while it will enable the soldier to offer, if not a bolder, at least a more formidable front, to the foe, and save him from many of the hazards of the march in which more die than on the field of battle!

Though the subject has as yet received too little scientific attention, there can be no doubt that the hair generally has a further important function to perform in regulating the electricity which is so intimately connected with the condition of the nerves.

I have reserved to the last the curious fact, which in itself is perfectly conclusive as to the protecting office of the Beard, and explains why its hair has additional provision for its nourishment; and this fact is, that while the hair of the head usually falls off with the approach of age, that of the Beard, on the contrary, continues to *grow* and *thicken* to the latest period of life. He must be indeed insensible to all evidence of design, who does not acknowledge in this a wise and beneficent provision, especially when he connects with it the other well-known fact, that the skull becomes denser, and the brain less sensitive, while the parts shielded by the Beard are more susceptible than ever, and have less vitality to contend with prejudicial influences.

Before proceeding further it may be as well briefly to answer the question, why, if Beards be so necessary for men, women have no provision of the kind? The reason I take to be this, that they are women, and were consequently never intended to be exposed to the hardships and difficulties men are called upon to undergo. Woman was made a help meet for man, and it was designed that man should in return, protect her to the utmost of his power from those external circumstances which it is his duty boldly to encounter. Her hair grows naturally longer, and in the savage state she is accustomed to let it fall over the neck and shoulders. The ancient Athenian and Lombard women are even said to have accompanied their husbands to the battle-field with their hair so arranged as to imitate the Beard. In more civilized society, various contrivances are resorted to by the gentler sex for protection, which would be utterly unsuitable to the sterner. In saying this I do not include the present absurd bonnet, which seems purposely contrived to expose rather than shield the fair, and to excite our pity and cause us to tremble while we cannot but admire!

Two curious exceptional cases of bearded women must not be passed over; one, that of a female soldier in the army of Charles XII, who was taken at the battle of Pultowa, where she had fought with a courage worthy of her Beard: the other, that of Margaret of Parma, the celebrated Regent of the Netherlands, who conceived that her Beard imparted such dignity to her appearance, that she would never allow a hair of it to be touched.

ARTISTIC DIVISION

NOT ONLY was the Beard intended to serve the important purposes just described; but, combining beauty with utility, to impart manly grace and free finish to the male face. To its picturesqueness, Poets and Painters, the most competent judges, have borne universal testimony. It is indeed impossible to view a series of bearded portraits, however indifferently executed, without feeling that they possess dignity, gravity, freedom, vigour, and completeness; while in looking on a row of razored faces, however illustrious the originals, or skilful the artists, a sense of artificial conventional bareness is experienced.

Addison gives vent to the same notion, when he makes Sir Roger de Coverley point to a venerable bust in Westminster Abbey, and ask "whether our forefathers did not look much wiser in their Beards, than we without them?" and say, "for my part, when I am in my gallery in the country, and see my ancestors, who many of them died before they were of my age, I cannot forbear regarding them as so many old Patriarchs, and at the same time looking upon myself as an idle smock-faced young fellow. I love to see your Abrahams, your Isaacs, and your Jacobs, as we have them in the old pieces of tapestry, with Beards below their girdles that cover half the hangings." The knight added, "if I would recommend Beards in one of my papers, and endeavour to restore human faces to their ancient dignity, upon a month's warning he would undertake to lead up the fashion himself in a pair of whiskers." In reference to this last allusion it may be as well to state, that the word whisker is frequently used by earlier authors to denote the moustache, and that in Addison's time, a mass of false hair was worn, and the head and face close shaven.

To shew that it is the Beard alone that causes the sensation we have alluded to, look at two drawings on exactly the same original outline, of a Greek head of Jupiter, the one with, the other without the Beard! What say you? Is not the experiment a sort of "occular demonstration" in favor of nature, and a justification of art and artists? See how the forehead of the bearded one rises like a well-supported dome—what depth the eyes acquire—how firm the features become—how the muscular angularity is modified—into what free flowing lines the lower part of the oval is resolved, and what gravity the increased length given to the face imparts.

As amusing and instructive pendants, take two drawings of the head of a lion, one with and the other without the mane. You will see how much of the majesty of the king of the woods, as well as that of the lord of the earth, dwells in this free flowing appendage. By comparing these drawings with those of Jupiter, you will detect, I think, in the head of the lion whence the Greek sculptor drew his ideal of this noble type of godlike humanity.

Since this idea struck me, Mr. John Marshall, in a lecture at the Government School of Practical Art, has remarked, "that nature leaves nothing but what is beautiful uncovered, and that the masculine chin is seldom sightly, because it was *designed to be covered*, while the chins of women are generally beautiful." This view he supported by instancing, "that the bear, the rabbit, the cat, and the bird, are hideous to look upon when deprived of their hairy and feathery decorations: but the horse, the greyhound, and other animals so sparingly covered that the shape remains unaltered by the fur, are beautiful even in their naked forms." This argument, it seems to me, applies with greater force to the various ages of man. In the babe, the chin is exceedingly soft, and its curve blends into those of the face and neck: in the boy it still retains a feminine gentleness of line, but as he advances to the youth, the bones grow more and more prominent, and the future character begins to stamp itself upon the form: at the approach of manhood, the lines combining with those of the mouth become more harsh, angular, and decided; in middle age, various ugly markings establish themselves about both, which in age are rendered not only deeper, but increased in number by the loss of the teeth and the falling in of the lips, which of course distorts all the muscles connected with the mouth. Such, however, is the force of prejudice founded on custom, that people who sink themselves to the ears in deep shirt collars, and to the chin in starched cravat and stiffened stock, muffle themselves in comforters till their necks are as big as their waists; nay do not demur some of them to be seen in that abomination of ugliness—that huge black patch of deformity—a respirator, have still sufficient face left to tell us that the expression of the countenance would be injured by restoring the Beard!

A word, therefore, on the expression of Bearded faces. The works of the Greeks,* the paintings of the old Masters,

---

* Elmes says, "The Beard in Art has an ideal character as an attribute, and distinguished by its undulating curl the Beard of Jupiter Olympius from that of Jupiter Serapis (who has a longer and straighter Beard) the lank Beard of Neptune and the river Gods, from the short and frizzly Beards of Hercules, Ajax, Diomede, Ulysses, &c."

but above all the productions of the pencil of Raphael, justly styled "the Painter of Expression," is a sufficient general answer to this ill-considered charge. It would indeed be strange if He who made the male face, and fixed the laws of every feature—clothing it with hair, as with a garment, should in this last particular have made an elaborate provision to mar the excellency of His own work! Nothing indeed but the long effeminizing of our faces could have given rise to the present shaven ideal—to the forgetfulness of the true standard of masculine beauty of expression, which is naturally as antipodal as the magnetic north and south poles, to that of female loveliness, where delicacy of line, blushing changeable colour, and eyes that win by seeming not to wish it, are charms we all feel, and at the same time understand how inappropriate they are when applied to the opposite sex; where the bold enterprizing brow – the deep penetrating eye—the daring, sagacious nose, and the fleshy but firm mouth, well supported on the decided projecting chin, proclaim a being who has an appointed path to tread, and hard rough work to do, in this world of difficulties and ceaseless transition.

So much for the general charge; if we examine the separate features, there can be no question that the upper part of the face—the most godlike portion—where the mind sits enthroned, gains in expression by the addition of and contrast with the Beard; the nose also is thrown into higher relief, while the eyes acquire both depth and brilliancy. The mouth, which is especially the seat of the affections, its surrounding muscles rendering it the reflex of every passing emotion, owes its general expression to the line between the

lips—the key to family likeness; and this line is more sharply defined by the shadow cast by the moustache, from which the teeth also acquire additional whiteness, and the lips a brighter red. Neither the mouth nor chin are, as we have said, unsightly in early life, but at a later period the case is otherwise. There is scarcely indeed a more *naturally* disgusting object than a beardless old man (compared by the Turks to a "plucked pigeon") with all the deep-ploughed lines of effete passions, grasping avarice, disappointed ambition, the pinchings of poverty, the swollen lines of self-indulgence, and the distortions of disease and decay! Now the Beard, which, as the Romans phrased it, "buds" on the face of youth in a soft downiness in harmony with immature manliness, and lengthens and thickens with the progress of life, keeps gradually covering, varying, and beautifying, as the "mantling ivy" the rugged oak, or the antique tower, and by playing with its light free forms over the harsher characteristics, imparts new graces even to decay, by heightening all that is still pleasing, veiling all that is repulsive.

The colour of the Beard is usually warmer than that of the hair of the head, and reflection soon suggests the reason: The latter comes into contact chiefly with the forehead, which has little colour; but the Beard grows out of the face where there is always more or less. Now nature makes use of the colours of the face in painting the Beard—a reason by the bye for not attempting to alter the original hue, and carries off her warm and cold colours by that means. Never shall I forget the circumstance of a gentleman with high colour, light brown hair, full whiskers of a warm brown, deepening into a warm black, and good looking, though his features, especially the nose, were not regular—taking a whim into his head to shave off his whiskers. Deprived of this fringe, the colour of his cheeks looked spotty, his nose forlorn and wretched, and his whole face like a house on a hill-top exposed to the north east, from which the sheltering plantations had been ruthlessly removed.

The following singular fact in connection with the colour of the Beard, I learnt in chance conversation with a hairdresser. Observing that persons like him with high complexion and dark hair, had usually a purple black beard: he said, "that's true, sir," and told me he had "found in his own Beard, and in those of his customers, distinct red hairs intermingled with the black," just as it is stated that in the grey fur of animals there are distinct rings of white and black hairs. This purplish bloom of a black Beard is much admired by the Persians; and curiously enough they produce the effect by a red dye of henna paste, followed by a preparation of indigo.

There is one other point connected with colour which ought not to be omitted. All artists know the value of white in clearing up colours. Now let any one look at an old face surrounded by white hair, whether in man or woman, and he will perceive a harmonizing beauty in it, that no artificial imitation of more youthful colours can possibly impart. In this, as in other cases, the natural is the most becoming.

Permit me to conclude this section of my lecture by reminding all who wish to let their Beards grow, that there is a law above fashion, and that each individual face is endowed with its individual Beard, the form and colour of which is determined by similar laws to those which regulate the tint of the skin, the form and colour of the hair of the head, eyebrows, and eyelashes; and therefore the most becoming, even if ugly in itself, to their respective physiognomies. What suits a square face, will not suit an oval, and a high forehead demands a different Beard to a low one. Leave the matter therefore to nature, and in due season the fitting form and colour will manifest themselves. And here parties who have never shaved have this great advantage over those who have yielded to the unnatural custom, that hair will only be visible, even when present, in its proper place, be better in character and colour, and more graceful in its form.

And now, ladies and gentlemen, as all history we are told grew out of fable, allow me, as a sort of intermezzo, to preface my history by "a Fable for the Times."

> An Ape, one day, said to a Goat,
> "Why wear that nasty ugly Beard?
> I'll shave you for a quarter groat
> Cleaner than Sheep was ever shear'd."
>
> "Thank you, Sir Ape!" the Goat replied,
> "I'll think of it." To court he ran,
> Where he the foplings busy spied
> Effacing ev'ry mark of man:
>
> Thinking to win the softer sex
> By making themselves *softer* still.
> "Ah!" says our Goat, "ah! ah! I'feggs,
> I'll be in fashion, that I will!"
>
> He seats himself, the Ape's not slow,
> But tucks the cloth in, and then lathers;
> When lo! stalk'd by a goodly row,
> A solemn train of old Church Fathers!

With these came Doctors of each Art,
And each one pointed to his Beard!
Our Goat sprang up, with sudden start,
Like one whom conscience makes afeard.

"O Ape! this man's a creature brave,
To whom we all like slaves submit;
Bearded to-day—t'morrow he'll shave,
Then where's the good of his boasted wit!

"There's your apron! take your basin!
Tis best to abide by nature's rule:
His Beard no Goat will see disgrace in,
Whom nature did not make a fool!"

MORAL
Let your Beards grow in their natural shapes,
God made you all *Men*, don't make yourselves *Apes!*

HISTORICAL SURVEY

EGYPTIANS

HAVING seen that the Beard is a natural feature of the male face, and that the Creator intended it for distinction, protection, and ornament, let us turn lightly over the pages of history and examine the estimation in which it has been held at various times among the leading people, ancient and modern.

The first nation which suggests itself is the Egyptian, and very peculiar forms of Beard were assigned by them on their monuments to their gods, kings, and common people. That of the gods is curled and the length of the oval of the face: that of the kings is shaped like an Egyptian doorway, and three fourths of the same standard: of which the people's is one fourth and nearly square. This appendage seems from the appearance of an attaching band to have been frequently artificial, and probably the Egyptians, who, as you may see by the wig in the British Museum, wore false hair, also wore false Beards. Some have supposed the forms alluded to, to be mere symbols of the male sex on the monuments; but this notion is disproved by male persons being represented without them. That they were occasionally so used, however, is clear from the kingly Beard on that symbol of royalty the Sphynx.

The priests of this ancient nation are stated to have removed every hair from the body thrice a week; and they ultimately

compelled the people to shave both their heads and faces; and all slaves and servants, though foreigners, were obliged to do the same. That this arose from some superstitious notion of cleanliness, is confirmed by the remark of Herodotus, "that no Egyptian of either sex, would on any account kiss the lips of a bearded Greek, or make use of his knife, spit, or caldron, or taste the meat of an animal which had been slaughtered by his hand."

In times of mourning, however, the Egyptians allowed the hair of the head and Beard to grow in token of grief.

JEWS

Such was the practice of the Egyptians; and it is highly important to take the Jews next, because at the period of our first knowledge of them as a people, they appear in bondage to the former nation; and it is now generally believed that most of the usages established by Moses had more or less reference to Egyptian customs, from which he was desirous of weaning them. As might be expected from the inspired Lawgiver, whose sublime books start with the grand assertion, that man was made "in the express image of God," any attempt to alter the natural features of the "human face divine," was denounced and emphatically interdicted. Twice is the commandment issued—first to the whole people, "thou shalt not mar the corners of thy Beard," in other words, thou shalt not alter the form thereof, which I thy God have appointed! Then to the Priests, with the addition, that they should not make baldness upon their heads. It is of the utmost consequence to recall the superstitious practice of the Egyptian Priests, and to remember that Moses issued this command to the Aaronites, fresh from Egypt, because it most convincingly shews that the practice of shaving, even when resorted to with the view of pleasing the Deity, by an extreme degree of external purity, in approaching His mysterious presence, was directly and most absolutely forbidden. It is as if God had said, "What art thou, O man! who thinkest in thy vain imagination that I, thy Creator, knew not how to fashion thee! and blasphemously supposest that thou canst please me, by superstitiously sacrificing what I, in my Almighty wisdom, had endowed thee with, for protection and ornament!" And, as if to mark the distinction more strongly, Moses enjoined in the strictest manner every ordinary and natural method of purifying the person.

It cannot but be instructive to note, that thus on the very threshhold of history, we have two customs so opposite brought into contrast—the one strongly condemned, the other most awfully sanctioned. And it is the more necessary to mark this, because there are many religious persons who have by custom acquired the Egyptian notion, and forgotten its emphatic condemnation. There are many who, though told that certain diseases to which the more active of the clergy are specially liable, might be prevented and may be cured; by simply wearing the Beard, will still insist upon their ministers paying the penalty invariably attaching to a violation of God's laws, because their prejudices lead them to fancy a smooth face rather than a manly one.

As further confirmation of our idea that the object of this law of Moses was to prevent any of the natural features from being materially altered—he objected not to trimming the Beard, which was a common Jewish practice—is to be found in the first verse of the 14th chapter of Deuteronomy, where the people are commanded not to shave their eyebrows; which was a customary mark of grief among some bearded nations. The Jews too, unlike the Persians and others, instead of shaving the Beard in time of mourning—though in the violence of oriental grief they sometimes plucked it—usually left it merely untrimmed or veiled, till the days of mourning were passed.

You all remember the fearful vengeance David took when his ambassadors were disgraced by shaving their Beards.

The Beard continued to be worn in all its glory by these chosen people, and it would be impossible for us to imagine to ourselves the appearance of any of their patriarchs, judges, priests, prophets, or mature kings—or of the sublime founder of our religion—or of the chosen twelve—save the youthful John, without this venerable and venerated feature. What painter would dare such an offence to our most sacred associations, as to represent any of these with the smirking smoothness of razored neatness!

That in Mahomet's time, the Jews still held to their primitive custom, is evident from that lawgiver's command to his followers to clip the whiskers and Beard, in order to distinguish themselves from the Jews. Indeed the latter, in every way most remarkable people, have clung to the prescribed custom with all the force of religious feeling and firm conviction. And however in modern times some of the laity, impelled by a desire to mix unobserved amongst the populations of Western Europe, may have sacrificed conviction to convenience, their Rabbis have remained invariably consistent in their testimony to truth and nature; and one of the most enduring impressions of my youth is the remembrance of the Chief Rabbi Herschel treading the streets of London, like the last of the prophets, in dark robes, with long pale face and flowing Beard,

> And eyes, whose deep mysterious glow,
> Disdainful of each fleeting show,
> Dwelt in the old and sacred past,
> Or Seer-like scann'd the future, vast.

ASSYRIANS AND BABYLONIANS

The Assyrians and Babylonians, as we know from the researches and discoveries of Layard and others, wore highly ornamental Beards, in which they were followed by the ancient Persians, and the bands appearing on them were of gold.

PERSIANS, ARABS, AND TURKS

The ancient Arabs, like their kindred, the Jews, were Bearded, and like them also they have preserved their Beards intact, though their faith has more than once changed. From Mahomet's time we may class them for our purpose with the Turks and Persians, since all have manifested the same respect for the Beard, looking upon it as the perfection and completion of man's countenance and the type of freedom; and shaving as a mark of debasement and slavery.* Mahomet, who sanctioned dyeing the Beard, preferred that it should be

---

* "It is customary to shave the Ottoman Princes as a mark of subjection to the reigning Sultan; and those who serve in the Seraglio have their Beards shaven as a sign of servitude, and do not suffer it to grow till the Sultan has set them at liberty."—*Burder's Oriental Customs*. Volney says, "At length Ibrahim Bey suffered Ali his page to let his Beard grow, i.e. gave him his freedom, for among the Turks to want the Beard is thought only fit for slaves and women."

of a cane colour, which was the hue assigned by tradition to Abraham's. One of the points of Persian heresy is preferring a black Beard, and a particular cut; and about this hair-splitting difference, they once waged a cruel war with the Uzbec Tartars, in which they were accustomed to lay their enemies' Beards as trophies at the feet of the Shah.

As instances of respect paid to the Beard, we may cite the common Mahomedan oath "by the Beard of the Prophet!" and the form of supplication, "by your Beard, or the life of your Beard." The Turks will point to theirs and say, "do you think this venerable Beard could lie?" And a man's testimony used to be so much measured by his Beard, that in hiring a witness, length of this appendage was an indispensable qualification. To touch another's Beard, unless to kiss it respectfully, is considered by all these people a great insult. When two friends meet, to kiss it, sometimes on both sides, answers to our shake of the hand—how are you? and "may God preserve your Beard!" is a form of invoking a blessing on a friend. In the bosoms of their families the Beard is treated as an object of reverential fondness—wife and children kissing it with the most tender and respectful affection. To express high value for a thing, they say, "it is worth more than one's Beard."*

"Shame on your Beard!" is a term of reproach, and "I spit on your Beard!" an expression of the most profound contempt. When the Shah of Persia, in 1826, was speaking to our Ambassador, (Sir J. Malcolm,) concerning the Russians,

---

* Dr. Wolff says, Mahomed Effendi told him "that the Mahomedans believed that though Noah lived 1000 years, no hair of his blessed Beard fell off, or became white; while that of the Devil consists only of one long hair;" and the same Mahomed, wishing to compliment two midshipmen, "hoped they would some day have fine long Beards like himself."

to shew how low he esteemed them, he exclaimed, "I spit on their Beards!"*

To cut off the Beard is considered a deep disgrace and degradation. The noted Wahabee Chief Saoud was accustomed to shave the Beard as a punishment for the gravest offences. He had long wished to purchase the mare of a Sheikh of the Shahmanny tribe, but all his offers were rejected. A Sheikh of the Kahtans, however, having been sentenced to lose his hairy honors, when the barber appeared, exclaimed, "O Saoud, take the mare of the Shahmanny as a ransom for my Beard!" The offer was accepted, and a bargain struck with the owner of the mare for 2,500 dollars, which he declared he would not have taken, nor any other sum, had it not been to save the Beard of a noble Kahtan.

Even when disease or accident renders necessary the removal of the whole or part of the Beard, it is only at the last extremity that an Arab will yield; and then he lives secluded, or if obliged to go out, wears a thick black veil, until his chin can reappear "with all its pristine honours blushing thick upon it."

Almost every Mahomedan carries a comb with him for the sole purpose of arranging his Beard: this is often done, especially after prayers; when the devotee usually remains sitting on his heels and industriously using the comb. The hairs which fall are carefully collected, to be either buried

---

* Niebuhr says, "I once saw, in a caravan, an Arab highly offended at a man who had accidentally bespattered his Beard. It was with difficulty he could be appeased, even though the offender humbly asked his pardon, and kissed his Beard in token of submission." Though I avoided breaking the argument by its insertion under the account of the Jews, it may be interesting to state, that Moses, in Numbers, orders a man to be considered unclean for seven days, whose Beard has been defiled in this way; and that David could scarcely have devised a more efficient means to convince Achish of his madness, than the expedient he adopted of allowing his saliva to descend upon his Beard.

with the owner, or deposited previously in his tomb, after having been first separately broken in order to release the guardian angels.

To perfume and fumigate the Beard with incense is a common eastern custom.

In mourning, the Persians shave themselves; and Herodotus relates one instance when they also cropped the manes and tails of their horses in honor of their leader Mardonius.

One wiseacre of a Sultan is said to have shaved his Beard, saying "his councillors should never lead him by it, as they had done his forefathers!" forgetting that he had still left them the convenient handle of his nose—by which, as you know, ladies and gentlemen, people have been led from time immemorial. Let me hope, therefore, no one will cite this as an historical precedent for shaving.

He was fortunately succeeded by wiser men, and the Sultan is yet distinguished by a goodly Beard:' as is also the Shah of Persia, and all the Arabs and their Chiefs.

Greeks

The ancient Greeks were world-famous for their Beards. All Homer's heroes are bearded, and Nestor the Sage is described as stroking his as a graceful prelusion to an oration. Saturn, Jupiter, Neptune, Pluto, Mars, Vulcan, Mercury, are represented with Beards. Apollo is without, as an emblem of perpetual youth. Hercules and the demigods are also well furnished. And Æsculapius the God of Health,—significant

---

* It used to be considered one of the almost impossible feats of Chivalry to pluck a hair from the Sultan's Beard.—(May the Russians find it quite so!) The romance of Oberon is founded on this notion, and Shakespeare makes Benedict say in a spirit of bravado, "I'll fetch you a hair off the great Cham's Beard." (*i.e.* Khan of Tartary's Beard.)

fact!—is most abundantly endowed. The mother of Achilles, when supplicating Jupiter, touches his Beard with one hand, with the other his knee.

As might be supposed from their hardy characteristics, the Spartans especially cherished the Beard. When one Nicander was asked why? he replied, "because we esteem it the ornament that preeminently distinguishes man." It being demanded of another why he wore so *long* a Beard? his noble reply was, "Since it is grown white, it incessantly reminds me not to dishonor my old age."* Plutarch, after mentioning the bushy hair and Beard of the Spartan commander Lysander, says, "that Lycurgus was of opinion that abundance of hair and Beard made those who were fair, more so, and those who were ugly, more terrible to their enemies." Regarding shaving as a mark of slavish servitude, they compelled their chief magistrates to shave their upper lips during their term of office, to remind them that though administrators of the laws, they were still subject to them.

The Greeks in general continued to wear the Beard till the decay of Athenian virtue brought that free state into subjection to the Macedonian Conqueror, who, according to Plutarch, ordered his soldiers to shave, lest their Beards should afford a handle to their enemies. This must have been when he was in one of his drunken fits, or he might have had

---

* The Rev. John More, of Norwich, a worthy clergyman in Elizabeth's reign, who is said to have had the longest and largest Beard of any Englishman of his time, seems to have chosen this Spartan for his model; since when asked to give a reason for it he replied, "that no act of his life might be unworthy of the gravity of his appearance." And Baudinus, quoted by Pagenstecher, says Frederick Taubman, the celebrated German wit, humourist, and theologian, being asked the same question answered, "in order that whenever I behold these hairs, I may remember that I am no vile coward or old woman, but a man, called Frederick Taubman."

them trimmed like the old Greek warriors.* Be that as it may, Greek freedom and Greek Beards expired together.

Diogenes, contemporary with Alexander, once asked a smooth-chinned voluptuary whether he quarrelled with nature for making him a man instead of a woman? And Phocion rebuking one who courted the people and affected a long Spartan Beard, said to him, "if thou needs must flatter, why didst thou not clip thy Beard?"

It is a curious fact for those who resolve civilization into shaving, that the only parties in ancient Greece who retained their Beards under all changes were the Philosophers, or lovers of wisdom—they with whom all that distinguished Greek intellect was a special study and profession; who were in fact the most civilized portion of the community.

From the time of the Emperor Justinian the Greeks resumed the Beard, which was worn by all the Greek Emperors down to the last, the unfortunate Paleologus, who died fighting bravely at the taking of Constantinople by the Turks. It was by these Emperors regarded as an ensign of royalty—an attribute of kingly majesty.

ETRUSCANS—ROMANS

The Etruscans represented their gods with Beards, and wore them themselves; as did the Romans. Every schoolboy recollects the awe inspired to the invading Gauls when, on

---

* That the Beard, however, sometimes afforded a handle to an enemy in ancient times, when swords, especially the Greek, were very short, is admitted. And I possess an engraving from one of Raphael's Vatican Cartoons, where one soldier is represented in the act of cutting down another whom he has seized by the Beard. He must be a poor master of his weapon, however, who in modern times would allow a man to grasp his Beard without being hewn down or run through in the process.

entering the Senate-house, they saw the conscript Fathers sitting calm and immovable as the gods, for which the Barbarians at first view took them, till one bolder than the rest plucked at the Beard of the noble Marcus Papirius, who by indignantly raising his staff, unconsciously gave the signal for the murder of himself, and his venerable compatriots.

During all the best ages of the Republic, while the old Roman virtue retained something of its original vigour, and before it had been sapped and undermined by the imported vices and effeminate customs of conquered nations, Rome's statesmen, heroes, priests and people all wore, and all reverenced, the virile glories of the Beard!

It was not till the year of Rome 454, about three centuries before our era, that one of those corrupt Prætors, who usually returned laden with foreign gold, and pampered with foreign luxury, imported a stock of Barbers from Sicily; and that credulous gossip Pliny libels the younger Scipio Africanus by stating—calumnious on dit!—"that he was the first who shaved his whole Beard." This is just one of those instances where a foolish custom, like a bad piece of wit, is sought to be fathered on some world-renowned name.

Long after the above date, the Beard was only partially shaved or trimmed; and the same word (*tondere*) is sometimes used to mean either. Of course when once the fashion had set in, it was, as with us, considered unbecoming to wear a Beard; and Marcus Livius on his return from banishment, was compelled by the Censors to shave, before appearing in the Senate.

With the increasing growth of vice and effeminacy among this once hardy race, the decreasing Beard kept pace.* Cæsar, the real founder of the empire, by whom every kind of foppery and debauchery was indulged in as a mask to deep schemes of ambition, of course shaved;† and having done so, shaving continued to be the imperial fashion down to the time of Hadrian, (whose bold Roman head I exhibited, as the first restorer of manly beauty.) From his time most of the Emperors‡† wore it till Constantine, who shaved out of superstition. His father had a noble Beard.

Even after the custom of shaving was introduced, the first appearance of the Beard was hailed with joy, and usually about the time of assuming the toga; the "first fruits" of hair were solemnly consecrated—relict of previous respect—to some god, as in the case of Nero,§ who presented his in a golden box, set with jewels, to the Capitoline Jupiter.

---

* Besides shaving, the Romans as they progressed in luxurious effeminacy, used depilatories, tweezers and all sorts of contrivances to make themselves as little like men and as much like women as possible; and their satirists abound with passages impossible to quote with decency on the causes and consequences of this abrogation of the distinctive peculiarities of the two sexes.

† Suetonius says, "he was excessively nice about his body, that he was not only sheared and shaved, but plucked."

‡ Pagenstecher says, "one of the Emperors of Rome refused to admit to an audience certain Ambassadors of the Veneti, because they had no Beards."

§ The branch of the Roman family to which Nero belonged was called Enobarbus, coppercoloured or red Beard; and the legend of the family was, that the Dioscuri announced to one of their ancestors a victory, and to confirm the truth of what was said, stroked his black hair and Beard, and turned them red. Cn. Domitius, who was Censor with L. Crassus the orator, "took" says Pagenstecher, "too much pride in his," and Crassus fired away the following epigram upon it. *Quid mirum si barbam habet aeneam Domitius cum et os ferreum et cor habet plumbeum.* (Where's the wonder Domitius has a brazen Beard, when he has bones of iron and a heart of lead.)

Shakespeare (the unlearned!) who never loses a characteristic, makes his Enobarbus, (who was great grandfather of Nero, wore a Beard, as seen on his medals, and was a fine bold warrior,) speak thus of Antony, under the fascination of Cleopatra:—

LEP. Good Enobarbus, 'tis a worthy deed,
        And shall become you well, to entreat your Captain
        To soft and gentle speech.
ENO. I shall entreat him
        To answer like himself: if Cæsar move him,

Shaving in token of grief was the custom of the early Romans; when, however, that which had been considered a deprivation became a general fashion, the Beard was allowed to grow in time of sorrow, to denote personal neglect.*

The Roman Philosophers, like the Greek, cherished a long Beard as the emblem of wisdom. The following anecdote shews that it was sometimes a fallacious sign. One of the Emperors being pestered by a man in a long robe and Beard, asked him what he was. "Do you not see that I am a philosopher?" was the reply. "The cloak I see, and the Beard I see," said the Emperor, "but the philosopher, where is he?"

I must not conclude this notice of Roman customs without mentioning the instructive fact, that the slaves of the early Romans were shaved as a mark of servitude, and not allowed to wear the distinctive sign of a free man until emancipated. At a later period the slaves, as the most manly, wore the Beard, and only shaved when entitled to be put on a level with their debased and vicious masters!

Let Antony look over Cæsar's head,
And speak as loud as Mars. By Jupiter,
Were I the wearer of Antonius' Beard,
I would not shave't to day.

This passage evidently associates the Beard with manly determination, and shaving with the want of it, for subsequently Enobarbus speaks of Antony's effeminacy in these words:—
Our courteous Antony,
Whom ne'er the word of *No* woman heard speak,
Being barber'd ten times o'er, goes to the feast,
And for his ordinary pays his heart
For what his eyes eat only.

* Arcite in Chaucer's *Knight's Tale* devotes his Beard to Mars:—
And eke to this avow I wol me bind,
My Berd, my here that hangeth low adoun,
That never yet felt non offensioun
Of rasour, ne of shere, I wol thee yeve.

47

ECCLESIASTICAL HISTORY

A BRIEF glance at Ecclesiastical History will furnish one or two interesting matters. Most of the Fathers of the Church both wore and approved of the Beard. Clement, of Alexandria, says, "nature adorned man like the lion, with a Beard, as the index of strength and empire." Lactantius, Theodoret, St. Augustine, and St. Cyprian, are all eloquent in praise of this natural feature: about which many discussions were raised in the early ages of the Church, when matters of discipline necessarily engaged much of the attention of its leaders. To settle these disputes, at the 4th Council of Carthage, held AD 252, canon 44, it was enacted "that a clergyman shall *not cherish his hair nor shave his Beard*." (Clericus nec comam nutriat nec barbam radat.) And Bingham quotes an early letter, in which it is said of one who from a layman had become a clergyman, "his habit, gait, modesty, countenance, and discourse, were all *religious*, and *agreeably to these his hair was short and his Beard long*;" shewing that in those early times St. Paul was better understood than at a later date.

Subsequently the Beard was alternately commended to the clergy for its becoming gravity, or condemned from the ascetic notion that pride was apt to lurk in a fine Beard. In some of the monasteries lay members wore the Beard, while those in orders were shaved, and the hairs, remnant of an earlier superstition, devoutly consecrated to God with special prayers and imposing ceremonies.

49

One order of the Cistercians were specially allowed to wear their Beards, and were hence called *fratres barbati* or Bearded brethren.

The military orders of the Church, as the Knights of St. John and the Templars, were always full Bearded.

To touch the Beard, was at one time a solemnity by which a godfather acknowledged the child of his adoption.

One of the fertile sources of dispute between the Roman and Greek Churches has been this subject of wearing or not wearing the Beard. The Greek Church, with a firm faithfulness which does credit to its orthodoxy, has stood manfully by the early Church decisions and refused to admit any shaven saint into its calendar, heartily despising the Romish Church for its weakness in this respect. On the other hand, the Popes, to mark the distinction between Eastern and Western Christianity, early introduced statutes *de radendis barbis*, or concerning shaving the Beard. Here and there, however, a manly old fellow, like Pope Julius II, who made Michael Angelo sculpture him with a drawn sword in his hand, or a Cardinal, like Pole or Allen, and many Bishops, managed to believe that faith and nature might be reconciled by taking a comprehensive and truly Catholic view of both.

The leading English and German Reformers wore their Beards; (if Luther confined himself to a moustache, it was because his Monkish habit of shaving was too strong for him,) and most of the Martyrs to the Protestant Faith were burnt in their Beards.

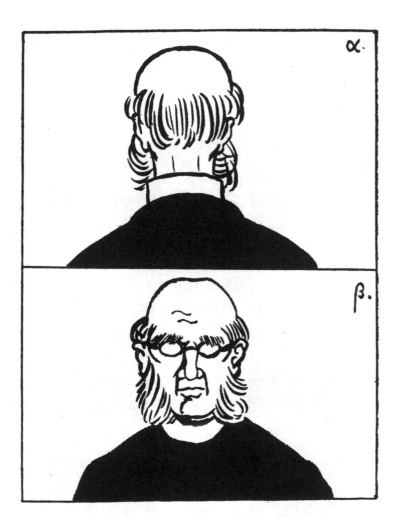

MODERN HISTORY

BRITONS

THE Britons "like their neighbours the Gauls"* (two of whose heads were shewn copied from Roman monuments) were Bearded, though, probably, for some purpose of distinction, their Chiefs, as stated by Cæsar and others, had merely an enormous twisted moustache. The Druids and their successors, the native British Clergy, regarded this natural covering as adding to their dignity and gracing their office and their age.††

SAXONS

The Anglo-Saxons brought their Beards with them which they preferred of the forked shape, and this again might be either two-pronged, or three-pronged, or plutonian and neptunian.

St. Augustine is figured with his Beard on his appearance to convert these Islands in the sixth century. His followers must soon have shaved, because a writer of the seventh century complains that "the Clergy had grown so corrupt as to be distinguished from the Laity less by their actions than by their want of Beards." The illustrious Alfred was so

---

* The Goths and Dacians, as seen on the Roman monuments, were Bearded; and the ancient Hungarians, Raumer states, wore long Beards adorned with gold and jewels. The Catti also were accustomed not to trim the hair of the head or Beard till they had proved their manliness by slaying an enemy in battle.

† One of the Legends of King Arthur mentions a giant who made "a great exhibition of domestic manufacture," consisting of a "cloak fringed with the Beards of kings."

careful of the Beards of his subjects, that he inflicted the then heavy fine of twenty shillings on any one maliciously injuring the Beard of another. The Danes who invaded this country were Bearded, Fosbrooke says, some of them wore Beards with six forks, and history mentions Sueno the fork-beard.*

During this period, the French monarchy was growing. Its first kings held the Beard as sacred, and ornamented it with gold. Their subjects were proud of it as marking them out to be free men in contradistinction to the degenerate Roman population. Alario touched the Beard of Clovis as a solemn mode of confirming a treaty, and acknowledging Clovis as his godfather. The Merovingian Dynasty were Bearded. Then came Charlemagne who swore by his Beard, as did Otho the Great and Barbarossa, Emperors of Germany, after him. The following story shows the faith of those early times in the sacredness of this form of adjuration. A peasant, who had sworn a false oath on the relics of two holy Martyrs, having taken hold of his Beard, as further confirmation, heaven to punish him, caused the whole to come off in his hand!

Charlemagne also enacted that any one who should call another red-beard or red-fox, should pay a heavy fine; a law explained by a prejudice embodied in two German proverbs:†

Of red-beard no good heard
Red beard—a knave to be feared

---

* Many princes have borne the title of Bearded—as the Greek Emperor Constantine Pogonatus, Count Godfrey, the Emperor Barbarossa, and Eberhard Duke of Wirtemberg in the reign of Maximilian, whose wisdom might truly be said to have grown with his Beard, and on whom the following verse was made:—
Hic situs est qui barba dedit cognomina Princeps,
Princeps Teutonici gloria magna soli.
(Here is a Prince whose Beard gave his surname,
A Prince the glory of the land Almayne.)

† *Rothbart nie gut wart*
Rothbart Schelmen art.

54

and carried to its climax in the anecdote of a Spanish nobleman, who, having accused a man of some crime, and the latter being proved innocent, exclaimed, "if he did not do it he was plotting it, for the rascal has a red beard!" Those who need consolation under this calumny, traceable probably to an old notion, derived from his name, that Judas Iscariot had a red beard, I am fortunately able to refer to a sermon* on that Arch-Traitor, full of wit, humor, pathos, and imagination, by the celebrated Abraham St. Clara, where red beards are nobly vindicated, and the following noted instances cited:—

—Several illustrious Romans,
—The Emperor Barbarossa;
—Hanquinus Rufus, King of the Goths;
—Bishops Gaudentius and Gandulfius;
—The Martyrs Dominicus, Maurinus, and Savinianus.

During the distractions to which Charlemagne's empire was subject after his decease, the Northmen appeared, and a band, under Rollo, having been converted and settled in what is now Normandy, became known in English History as the Normans; with whom an increasing intimacy having sprung up in the reign of Edward the Confessor (whose head was shewn from the Bayeux tapestry) a Norman party was gradually formed at court and Norman customs, one of which was shaving, partially adopted. Harold, as representative of the real old English party, wore his Beard as shown by a contemporary MS illuminator; but William the Conqueror, and most of his followers, are figured only with a moustache and their back hair close cropped or shaven. It was this

---

* Judas der Ertz. Schelm.

barbarous fashion that induced Harold's spies to report to their master that the invaders were an army of Priests.

William is said to have attempted to compel the sturdy Saxons to shave, but many of them left the kingdom rather than part with their Beards. In this, as in other matters, Anglo-Saxon firmness ultimately conquered the conquerors, and the Norman sovereigns gave in to the national custom. As early as Henry I, that is *only 44 years from William's landing*, we learn that Bishop Serlo met that monarch on his arrival in Normandy, and made a long harangue on the enormities of the times, especially long hair and bushy Beards, which he said they would not clip, lest the stumps should wound the ladies' faces. Henry, with repentant obedience, submitted his hairy honors to the Bishop, who with pious zeal, taking a pair of shears from his trunk, trimmed king and nobles with his own hand. This conduct of the Bishop is curiously illustrated by a contemporary decree of the Senate of Venice, of the year 1102, commanding all long Beards to be cut off in consequence of a Bull of Pope Paschal II, denouncing the vanity of long hair, founded on a misinterpretation of 1st Corinthians, xii, 14,* which applies only to the hair of the head. On this text a sermon might be written though scarcely preached, which would "a tale unfold, would harrow up the soul."†

The stout king Stephen wore his Beard, and a Saxon chronicler complains that in the civil wars of his time, in order to extort the wealth of peaceable people, they were

---

* A writer in Dickens' *Household Words* says Pope Anacletus was the first who introduced the custom of shaving.

† In this and in other places I am obliged to leave under a veil of obscure allusion, arguments of thrilling force, not only from ancient but from our own history: matters not to be met with in ordinary histories; but too abundant in the pages of satirists and moralists, who were hardy enough to lash the prevalent follies and vices of the times in which they lived.

"hung up by their Beards;" a proof the latter were long and strong. Stephen's contemporary, Frederick the 1st of Germany, to prevent quarrelling, laid a very heavy fine on any one who pulled another's Beard.

Henry II is said to have had a vision in which all classes of his subjects reproached him in his sleep for his tyranny and oppression. A contemporary MSS. illuminator, having fortunately designed several cartoons, really much more expressive than some in the New Houses of Parliament, from which we learn that the faces of all classes of the people and of the Clergy then appeared as nature made them, I selected one, representing the leaders of the distressed agriculturalists of that remote period, because while it illustrated my subject, it seemed to possess great interest for that patient and much enduring class. One could almost imagine the stout fellow with the one-sided Saxon spade, to be urging on the heroes with the pitchfork and scythe, nearly in the words of Marmion,

Charge, Sibthorp,* charge! On, Stanley, on!

Henry's Queen Eleanor had been previously the wife of Louis VII, of France, who having been persuaded by his Priests to shave off his Beard, so disgusted Eleanor that she obtained a divorce.†

---

* I trust my honest and uncompromising brother Beard will pardon the liberty I have taken with his name. No one can be a more sincere admirer than myself of the manly way in which he maintains his opinions on all occasions, and the humorous kindness of disposition which renders him beloved in private and in public. I should always esteem him as a public man, were it only for his long and single-handed fight against that economical iniquity—that suicidal tax on prudence and foresight, and bounty on improvidence—the Fire Insurance Duty!

† "She had," says D'Israeli, "for her marriage dower the rich province of Poitou and Guyenne; and this was the origin of those wars which for 300 years ravaged France, and cost the French three million of men. All which probably had never occurred had Louis VII not been so rash as to crop his head and shave his Beard, by which he became so disgustful in the eyes of our Queen Eleanor."

Richard the Lion-hearted was Bearded like a lion, and though he was so absorbed in the Crusades that he did not redress, yet he acknowledged the justice of the complaints of the celebrated Longbeard, "Earl of London and King of the Poor," who did honor to his Beard by resisting oppression, and perished, after an heroic struggle, the victim of cowardice and treachery. The monuments of Roger, Bishop of Sarum, and Andrew, Abbot of Peterborough, shew that Bishops wore the Beard, and Abbots and Monks shaved in this reign.

John had what was called "a Judas Beard," of which his actions were every way worthy. Fortunately, the bold Barons outbearded him, and Magna Charta was the result. His son, Henry III, had a moderate Beard, and the longest reign till George III. Edward I, shewed the Scots what a long Beard could do with long shanks, and a long head to back it.* This king has been called the English Justinian, both he and the Roman Emperor being noted for improving the laws, and cherishing their Beards. Edward the 2nd's Beard, like his character, was more ornamental than strong, and his reign is chiefly memorable for the composition of that favorite old song quoted by Shakespeare, "Tis merry in hall, when Beards wag all!"

Edward the 3rd's bold Beard spread terror in Scotland and France, and that of his son, the Black Prince—young as he died—was an apt type of his "prowess in the tented field."

Richard the 2nd, with all his faults, was neither deficient in Beard nor in courage—the latter shewn in his meeting with

---

* No true Scotchman would pardon me if I omitted to note that the brave Wallace had "a most brave Beard."

Wat Tyler, and his defence against his assassins. Henry IV, the crafty Bolingbroke, had a chin cover, in whose every curl lurked an intrigue, of which his son, Henry V, who was made of other metal, was so ashamed, we presume, that he wore in penitence a shaven chin throughout his ten years' reign, as may be seen by his monument in Westminster Abbey, the remains of which still exist.

Shaving continued partially in fashion in Henry the 6th's reign, who himself in later life was Bearded like a Philosopher, accustomed to moralize over the ups and downs of life, of which he had no common share. Edward the 4th shaved out of foppery; as did that smooth-faced rascal, Richard III, who "could smile and smile and be a villain." Henry the 7th shaved himself and fleeced his people.

As may be seen in MSS. illuminations, and as we read in Chaucer and elsewhere, the majority of the people stuck to their Beards, uninfluenced by the fluctuations of court fashions. The poet, who was born in Edward the 3rd's time, and died in Henry the 4th's, speaks of "the merchant's forked Beard;" "the Franklin's white as a daisy;" "the shipman's shaken by many a tempest;" "the miller's red as a fox, and broad as though it were a spade;" the Reeve's close trimmed; the Sompnour's piled; and ends by a contemptuous allusion to the Pardonere with his small voice:

No Beard had he, nor never none should have,
As smooth it was as it were newe shave, &c.

Henry VIII, as you may still see on many sign boards, for which his bluff, bloated face is so well adapted, had his Beard close clipped. Once he swore to Francis the 1st that he would never cut it till he had visited the latter, who swore the same;

and when long Beards had become the fashion at the French Court Sir Thomas Bulleyn was obliged to excuse Henry's bad faith, by alleging that the Queen of England felt an insuperable antipathy to a bushy chin, which, from the known considerate conduct of Henry to his wives, must have been a very plausible plea! Sir T. Moore shaved previous to his imprisonment. His Beard being then allowed to grow, he conceived such an affection for it, that before he laid his head on the block he carefully put it on one side, remarking "that it at least was guiltless of treason, and ought not to be punished."

Although Francis I, and his Court, cherished their Beards, the Chancellor Duprat advised the imposition of a tax on the Beards of the clergy, and promised the king a handsome revenue. The bishops and wealthier clergy paid the tax and saved their Beards; but the poorer ministers were not so fortunate. In the succeeding reign, the clergy determined on revenge; so when Duprat (son of the Chancellor) was returning in triumph from the council of Trent, to take possession of the bishopric of Claremont, the dean and canons closed the brass gates of the chancel, through which they were seen armed with shears and razor, soap and basin, and pointing to the statutes, "de radendis barbis." Notwithstanding his remonstrances, they refused to induct him unless he sacrificed his Beard, which was the handsomest of his time. He is said to have retired to his castle, and died of vexation.

In the same reign, John de Morillers was also objected to by the Chapter of Orleans; but the cunning fellow produced a letter from the king stating, that the statutes must be dispensed with in his case, as his majesty intended to employ him in countries where he could not appear without a Beard.

At the court of the rival of Francis, Charles the 5th, who had himself a right royal covering to his chin, lived John Mayo, his painter, a very tall man, but with a Beard so long, that he could stand upon it; and in which he took much pride, suspending it by ribbons to his button-hole. Sometimes this mass of hair, by command of the Emperor, was unfastened at table, and doors and windows being thrown open, the imperial mind took intense delight in seeing it blown into the faces of his grimacing courtiers. Another noted German Beard was that of a merchant of Braunau in Bavaria, which was so long, that it would have draggled on the ground, had it not been incased by its proud owner in a beautiful velvet bag.*

The promising Edward the 6th died before his Beard developed; his sister Mary's husband had one of the true Spanish cut.

In the time of "good Queen Bess," when "The grave Lord Chancellor† led the dance, And seal and mace tripped down

---

* Southey in "The Doctor" mentions the Beard of Dominico d'Ancona, as the crown or King of Beards,

A Beard the most singular

Man ever described in verse or prose

and of which Berni says, "that the Barber ought to have felt less reluctance in cutting the said Dominico's throat, than in cutting off so incomparable a Beard." But Southey is outdone by a story told by Dr. Ehle in his work on the hair, where mention is made of two seven-foot giants with Beards down to their toes, at the court of one of the German sovereigns. They both fell in love with the same woman, and their master decided that whichever should succeed in putting his rival into a sack, should have the maiden. One of them sacked the other after a long duel before the whole court, and married the girl. That the pair lived happily afterwards, as the Novelists say, is proved by their having as many signs of affection as there are in the Zodiac; and it is worthy of remark, both physiologically and astrologically, that the whole twelve were born under one sign, Gemini.

† It surely will not be denied by any Judge of taste, that the Chancellor and other legal dignitaries would look more dignified in their own hair and with Beards of "reverend grey," than in the present absurd, fantastic, unnatural and unbecoming frosted ivy bushes, with a black crow's nest in the centre, in which Minerva might more readily mistake them for stray specimens of her favorite bird, the owl, than for learned, intelligent, and logical "sages of the law."

before him," she, who was no prude, and had a right royal sympathy with every thing manly and becoming, surrounded herself with men, who to the most punctilious courtesy, joined the most adventurous spirit; and the Beard, as might have been expected, grew and flourished mightily. Hence we are not surprised at the wonderful efforts made by her subjects in arms, and arts, and literature, so as to make her reign an era to which we look back with patriotic pride, and from which our best writers still draw as from a well of deep perennial flow.*

A feeble reflection of some of the heads of this period were exhibited on the walls of the lecture room, as the sagacious Burleigh; the adventurous Raleigh; the rash but brave Essex; Nottingham, the High Admiral who scattered the Armada; Gresham the Merchant Prince, who found his Beard no hindrance to business; and the Poet of Poets, whether ancient or modern, Shakespeare.

As might be expected, the dramatic literature of the time is full of allusions to that feature which men still honored and admired. Lear can find no more pathetic outburst of insulted majesty, in addressing his vile daughter Goneril, than the words—

---

* Although an attempt was made in this reign to restrain the growth of legal Beards by some pragmatical heads of Lincoln's Inn, who passed a resolution "that no fellow of that house should wear a Beard of above a fortnight's growth;" and although transgression was punished with fine, loss of commons, and final expulsion, such was the vigorous resistance to this act of tyranny, that in the following year all previous orders respecting Beards were repealed. *Percy Anecdotes.*

About the same time also in Germany the moustache was partially substituted for the Beard, as appears by Berckemej's 'Europ. Antiq. p. 294, who under the year 1564 says, the Archbishop Sigismund introduced in Magdeburgh the custom of shaving off the full Beard and wearing instead a moustache. The year in which this Beard-reformation (de-formation?) happened, was contained in this pentameter—

LONGA SIGISMVNDO BARBA IVBENTE PER IT.

(Sigismund commanding the long Beard perished in MDLVV(= x)IIII, or 1564)

62

Art not ashamed to look upon this Beard?

and when Regan insults the faithful Gloster, the latter exclaims—

By the kind Gods! 'tis most ignobly done
To pluck me by the Beard!

In a more mocking humour, Shakespeare makes Cressida say of Troilus's chin, "alas poor chin! many a wart is richer!" And Rosalind to Orlando, "I will pardon you for not having a neglected Beard, for truly your having in Beard is a younger brother's revenue."

Then as characteristics, we have the black, white, straw-colored, orange-tawney, purple-in-grain, and perfect yellow. The soldier Bearded like a pard; the justice with Beard of formal cut; the sexton's hungry Beard; and the Beard of the general's cut; and that fine passage, which you will pardon my quoting, if only to supply an obvious correction naturally lost sight of by *Beardless* commentators. If instead of the puerile conceit, *stairs* of sand, we read *layers* of sand, we not only restore metaphorical beauty but literal truth; for what is more deceitful than a layer of sand, and the Beard is "a layer of hair."

There is no one so simple but assumes
Some mark of virtue on his outward parts;
How many cowards, whose hearts are all as false
As *layers* of sand, wear yet upon their chins
The Beards of Hercules and frowning Mars,
Who, inward searched, have livers white as milk:
And these assume but valour's excrement
To make themselves redoubted.*

63

The witty Robert Green, published in 1592, a curious dialogue,[†] from which we get a glimpse into a Barber's shop of Queen Elizabeth's time. Cloth-breeches complains of the Barber's attention to Velvet-breeches in these terms.

His head being once dressed, which requires in combing and brushing some two hours; then being curiously washed with no worse than a camphor ball, you descend as low as his Beard, and ask whether he please to be shaven or no? whether he will have his peake cut short and sharp, amiable like an inamorato, or broad pendant like a spade, or le terrible, like a warrior or soldado? whether he will have his crates cut low like a juniper bush, or his subercles taken away with a razor? If it be his pleasure to have his appendices pruned, or his moustaches fostered to turn about his ears like the branches of a vine, or cut down to the lip with the Italian lash, to make him look like a half-faced baby in brass. These quaint terms Master Barber, you greet Master Velvet-breeches withal, and at every word a snap with your scissors and a cringe with your knee; whereas, when you come to poor Cloth-breeches, you either cut his Beard at your own pleasure, or else in disdain ask him if he will be trimmed

---

I am heartily grieved a Beard of your grave length
Should be so over-reach'd. (*The Fox.*)
In his *Alchemist* Subtle telling Drugger's fortune says—
This summer
He will be of the clothing of his company,
And next spring called to the scarlet.
FACE. What and so little Beard
[Pagenstecher asks "which was the city where Beard and foot made the magistrate?" and then proceeds gravely to relate that the inhabitants of Hardenberg had formerly the singular custom of electing their mayors or burgomasters by assembling it a round table, where while some of the town council were employed in inspecting their Beards, others were engaged in estimating their feet—the biggest Beard and largest foot being "called to the scarlet." And rightly too! for the Beard denoted authority and wisdom, and the large foot an understanding likely to take grave steps when needed. As containing a valuable hint to modern corporations to look well to the essential points of a mayor—too often overlooked—I trust this note upon note will be pardoned.]
† Quip for an Upstart Courtier.

with Christ's cut, round like the half of a Holland cheese, mocking both Christ and us.[*]

In the reign of James the 1st, Beards continued in fashion, and I extract two out of many passages from Beaumont and Fletcher's plays; the first being, not excepting even that of Butler's *Hudibras*, the most humourous description of a Beard in the language. A banished prince in disguise, having been elected "King of the Beggars" on account of his Beard; Higgen the Orator of the Troop proceeds in this fashion:—

> I then presaged thou shortly wouldst be king,
> And now thou art so. But what need presage
> To us, that might have read it in thy Beard,
> As well as he that chose thee! By the Beard
> Thou wert found out and marked for sovereignty.
> O happy Beard! but happier Prince, whose Beard
> Was so remarked as marked out our Prince
> Not bating us a hair. Long may it grow,
> And thick and fair, that who lives under it
> May live as safe as under Beggar's Bush,
> Of which *it* is the thing—*that* but the type.
> This is the Beard—the bush—or bushy Beard,
> Under whose gold and silver reign 'twas said,
> So many ages since, we all should smile!
> No impositions, taxes, grievances,
> Knots in a state, and whips unto a subject,
> Lie lurking in this Beard, but all combed out.

In his Queen of Corinth we learn that—

> The Roman T, your T-Beard is the fashion,
> And twifold doth express the enamoured courtier
> As full as your *fork carving* doth the traveller.

---

[*] Lilly in one of his Dramas makes a Barber say to his customer, "How, sir, will you be trimmed? Will you have a Beard like a spade or a bodkin? A penthouse on your upper lip or an ally on your chin? Your moustaches sharp at the ends like shoemaker's awls, or hanging down to your mouth like goat's flakes?"

The last line alluding to Coryate the traveller's recent introduction of the dinner-fork from Italy.

Of this Roman T-Beard another writer humorously says—

> The Roman T,
> In its bravery,
> Doth first itself disclose:
> But so high it turns,
> That oft it burns
> With the flame of a torrid nose.

and then adds—

> The soldier's Beard
> Doth match in this herd
> In figure like a spade;
> With which he will make
> His enemies quake
> To think their grave is made.

In 1610, died Henry IV, of France, whose Beard is said "to have diffused over his countenance a majestic sweetness and amiable openness;" his son Louis XIII,* ascending the throne while yet a minor, the courtiers and others, to keep him in countenance, began to shave, leaving merely the tuft called a mouche or royal. Sully, however, the famous minister of Henry, stoutly refused to adopt the effeminate custom. Being sent for to court, and those about the king having mocked at his old-fashioned Beard, the duke indignantly turned to Louis and said, "Sire! when your father of glorious memory did me the honor to hold a consultation on grave

---

* In this reign, whiskers however attained to a high degree of favour at the expense of the expiring Beard, and continued so under Louis XIV, who, with all the great men of his court, took a great pride in wearing them. In those days of gallantry, it was no uncommon thing for a lover to have his whiskers turned up, combed and pomatumed by his mistress; and a man of fashion was always provided with every necessary article for this purpose, especially whisker wax." *Percy Anecdotes.*

and important business, the first thing he did was to order out of the room all the buffoons and stage dancers of his court!" About this time also, Marshal Bassompierre having been released from a long imprisonment, declared the chief alteration he found was, "that the men had lost their Beards and the horses their tails."

Under our first Charles,* the sides of the face were often shaven, and the Beard reduced to the moustache, and a long chin-tuft, as in the portrait of that monarch, retaining however still some of its former gracefulness. As the contest grew hotter between Cavalier and Roundhead, doubtless some of the latter cropped chin as well as head; though others are said to have been so careful of their Beards, as to provide them with pasteboard night-caps to prevent the hairs being rumpled.

In one instance it was worn long for a sign, as we see by the following verse—

> This worthy knight was one that swore
> He would not cut his Beard,
> 'Till this ungodly nation was
> From kings and bishops cleared?
> Which holy vow he firmly kept,
> And most devoutly wore
> A grizzly meteor on his face,
> 'Till they were both no more.†

---

* D'Israeli quotes an auther of this reign, who in his "Elements of Education" says, "I have a favourable opinion of that young gentleman who is *curious in fine moustachios*. The time he employs in adjusting, dressing and curling them, is not lost time; *for the more he contemplates his moustachios, the more his mind will cherish and be animated by masculine and courageous notions.*"

D'Israeli also states, that the grandfather of Mrs. Thomas, the "Corinna of Dryden," was very nice in the mode of that age, his valet being some hours every morning in *starching his Beard and curling his whiskers*, during which time he was always read to.

† Taylor, the Water Poet, who lived from the end of Elizabeth to nearly the end of the Commonwealth, thus humorously describes the various fashions of this appendage.

Now a few lines to paper I will put,

Under Charles the 2nd, the Beard dwindled into the mere moustache, and then vanished. And when we consider the French apery of that un-English court, it is no wonder the Beard appeared too bold and manly an ensign to be tolerated. It went out first among the upper classes in London, and by slow degrees the sturdy country squires and yeomon also yielded their free honors to the slavish effeminate fashion, which, by the force of example, descended even to the working classes, on whom it imposed new burdens and some bodily diseases from which their hardy frames had been hitherto exempt. It is to be hoped, that when any one for the

---

Of men's Beards strange and variable cut,
In which there's some that take as vain a pride,
As almost in all other things beside:
Some are reaped most substantial like a brush,
Which makes a natural wit known by the bush;
And in my time of some men I have heard,
Whose wisdom hath been only wealth and Beard:
Many of these the proverb well doth fit,
Which says *bush* natural more hair than wit:
Some seem as they were starched stiff and fine,
Like to the bristles of some angry swine;
And some, to set their loves' desire on edge,
Are cut and prun'd like to a quickset hedge.
Some like a spade, some like a fork, some square,
Some round, some mow'd like stubble, some stark bare,
Some sharp, stilletto-fashion, dagger-like,
That may, with whispering, a man's eyes outpike,
Some with the hammer cut or Roman T,
Their Beards extravagant reform'd must be;
Some with the quadrate, some triangle-fashion,
Some circular, some oval in translation;
Some perpendicular in longitude,
Some like a thicket for their crassitude.
The heights, depths, breadths, triform, square, oval, round,
And rules geometrical in Beards are found.
[The stiletto Beard:
It makes me afeard
It is so sharp beneath:
For he that doth wear
A dagger in his face,
What must he wear in his sheath.
Old Author.
Who make sharp Beards and little breeches Deities.
Beaumont and Fletcher.]

future talks about the Beard being a *foreign* fashion, he will be reminded that it is a good old English natural fashion, and that the present custom of shaving was borrowed from France, at a time when we had no credit to borrow anything else, seeing that king, courtiers, and patriots, were all the pensioned dependents of the French monarch! The sooner therefore we cease to shave, the sooner shall we wipe out the remembrance of a disgraceful period of our history!

One amusing proof that the Beard continued to be worn by the country people after its decline about the court, is afforded by an anecdote of the notorious Judge Jeffries, who, in his browbeating way, thus addressed a party before him. "If your consience be as large as your Beard, fellow! it must be a swinging one." To which the witness replied, "If consciences be measured by Beards, I am afraid your lordship has none at all."

In 1700, Charles V ascended the throne of Spain, with a smooth chin; and his example was gradually followed, though the popular feeling has been condensed into the proverb—"Since we have lost our Beards, we have lost our souls;" and no one can question that loss of Beard and empire in that country have singularly coincided.

Two brief anecdotes will shew the sense of honor which formerly resided in Spanish and Portuguese Beards.

Cid Rai Diaz dying, a spiteful Jew stole into the room to do what he durst not when Diaz was alive—pluck the noble Spaniard's Beard! As he stooped for the purpose, the body started up and drew the sword lying in state by its side. The Jew fled horror-struck; the corpse smiled grimly, and resumed its repose; and the Jew turned Christian.

69

When the brave John de Castro had taken the Indian fortress of Dieu, being in want of supplies, he pledged one of his moustaches for a thousand pistoles, saying "all the gold in the world cannot equal the value of this natural ornament of my valour." The inhabitants of Goa, especially the ladies, were so struck with this magnaminous sacrifice, that they raised the money and redeemed the pledge.

The last European nation to lay aside the Beard was the Russian, in whose ancient code it was enacted that whoever plucks hair from another's Beard shall be fined four times as much as for cutting off a finger. Peter the Great (who always remained a semi-savage), like many other half-informed reformers, sought to accomplish his objects by arbitrary measures rather than by moral persuasion. Having, when in the west, seen unbearded faces, he jumped to the conclusion that absence of Beard was a necessary part of civilization; forgetting that a shaven savage is a savage still. He therefore ordered all his subjects to shave, imposing a tax of one hundred roubles on all nobles, gentlemen, tradesmen, and artizans, and a copeck on the lower classes. Great commotions were the result; but Peter was obstinate and made a crusade with scissors and razor, much resembling a Franco-African Razzia, which you know means a clean shave of everything with very dirty hands! Some, to avoid disgrace, parted with their Beards voluntarily, but all preserved the hairs to be buried in their coffins; the more superstitious believing that unless they could present theirs to St. Nicholas, he would refuse them admission to heaven as Beardless Christians.

One of the most difficult tasks was to deal with the army; in this, Peter proceeded with characteristic cunning.

Through the agency of the priests, the soldiers were told that they were going to fight the Turks, who wore Beards, and that their patron saint St. Nicholas would not be able to protect his beloved Russians, unless they consented to distinguish themselves by removing their Beards! You see how stale are the Czar's late tricks! Convinced by this pious fraud, the credulous soldiers obeyed the imperial mandate. The next war, however, was against the Swedes, and the soldiers, who had suffered severely from shaving, turned the tables upon the priests, and said, "the Swedes have no Beards, we must therefore let ours grow again, lest, as you say, the holy Nicholas should not know us!"

It is a note-worthy historical fact, which shews the danger arising from discarding the natural for the artificial, that as *Beards died out, false hair came in.* A mountain of womanish curls rested on the head, and was made to fall in effeminate ringlets over neck and shoulders, while the whole face was kept as smooth, and smug, and characterless as razor could make it. This renders it so disagreeable a task to look through a series of Kneller's portraits, who, clever as he was, could not impart the freedom and vigour of nature to this absurd fashion. A portrait of Addison,* was shewn as an illustration, because, as has been seen, though he complied with the mode, he was occasionally favored with visions of better times, past and to come.†

---

* I cannot refrain from alluding in a note to a curious fact. On the day this Lecture was given, a little boy was brought to look at the portraits just after they were hung. I said to him, "Edward, which face do you like best?" He instantly touched the portrait of Addison, and said, "that's the best woman," and "that's the best man!" pointing to the well-bearded face of Leonardo di Vinci.

† That Southey had the same compunctious visitings as Addison, appears clearly enough, for while in his Doctor he compares "shaving at home" with "slavery abroad;" states that "a good razor is more difficult to meet with, than a good wife;" denounces the practice "as

To the reign of false curls, succeeded that still more egregious outrage—that climax of coxcombry—powder, pomatum, and pigtails! The former to give the snows of age to the ruddy face of youth; the latter being, I suppose, an attempt of some bright genius to outdo nature,

> By hanging a stiff black tail behind,
> Instead of a flowing beard before,
> As if, by this ensign, the world to remind,
> How wise it had grown since old father Noah.

This was the period when every breeze was a Zephyr, every maid a Chloë, every woman a Venus, and every fat squinting child a Cupid! Later German critics even christen the writers of this school, "the Pigtail Poets."*

The first French Revolution made an end of all this trumpery, and though Alison and other professed historians have not classed the event among the good things flowing from that fearful flood of blood and blasphemy, it was not one of the least, and society cannot rejoice too much at being delivered from the example of systematic frippery,

---

preposterous and irrational," as "troublesome, inconvenient," and attended with "discomfort, especially in frosty weather and March winds;" places it on an equality with the curse pronounced on Eve; and concludes with the opinion that "if the daily shavings of one year could be put into one shave, the operation would be more than flesh and blood could bear;" he has nothing to say in favour of shaving, but that it encourages Barbers, compels the shaver to some moments of calm thought and reflection, and enables him to draw lessons from the looking glass that nobody with razor in hand ever thought of. These words in another place give a key to his real opinion. "If I wore a Beard," he writes, "I would cherish it as the Cid Campeador did his, for my pleasure. I would regale it on a Summer's day with rose-water, and without making it an idol, I should sometimes offer incense to it with a pastile, or with lavender and sugar. My children, when they were young enough for such blandishments, would have delighted to comb and stroke and curl it, and my grandchildren in their time would have succeeded to the same course of mutual endearment."

See also Leigh Hunt's humourous paper on Lie-abeds in the Indicator, where he calls "shaving a villainous and unnecessary custom."

* Seume, a German poet of a better school, in his travels says, "To-day I threw my powder apparatus out of window, when will the day come that I can send my shaving apparatus after it!"

frivolity, and tricked-out vice of the later French Sovereigns, imitated as they were by most of the petty puppet Princes of Germany—

Each lesser ape in his small way,
Playing his antics like the greater.

About the rise of the first Napoleon to power, a more simple, severe, and classic taste, was beginning to prevail, and this dictated a return to the Beard. Under the military despotism, however, of that Emperor, moustaches were forbidden to civilians, and the Beard restrained to that petty, hairy imitation of a reversed triangle—called after its reviver, who never personally wore it—the *imperial*, as if to denote to the people that they were to have the smallest possible share in the *empire*.

With every attempt at freedom on the Continent, the Beard re-appears; it was one of the most effective standards in the war of freedom, when Germany rose against Napoleon. In 1830, it was partially revived in France, and later still it has made many a perjured continental monarch* "quake and tremble in his capital," and reminded him that in spite of neglected promises and false oaths, the reign of injustice "hangs but on a hair," of which the police will not always be able to check the free growth.

---

* One hardly knows which is the most detestable, the canting hypocricy of Prussian constitutional pretence,—the more open poltroonery of Neapolitan despotism—or the paternal care to prevent even the buddings of free thought as in Austria, where I can state from my own knowledge that Schiller's works were seized as contraband on the Hungarian frontier, and a party in the Austrian service who had attempted to defend the conduct of the government at a Table d'Hôte was sent for by the head of the police, and when to excuse himself he alleged he was speaking for the government, was replied to—"Young man, the government want no defence—no discussion—and your wisest course is to be silent!"

I have now merely to notice very briefly, four modern objections to the Beard.

I. "*That it is less cleanly than shaving.*" To this, the answer is, that depends upon the wearer; and it will take less time to keep clean, than to shave, especially where, as in England, every one washes the face more than once a day. Besides, if this were an argument, we had better shave the head and eyebrows as well.

II. "*That it would take as much time to keep the Beard in order, as to shave.*" Supposing even it did, still there is a most important difference both in the two operations and in their results. For the process of combing and brushing the Beard, instead of being tedious, uncertain, and often painful, like shaving,* confers a positively delightful sensation, similar to that which one may imagine a cat to experience,

> When smoothing gently down its fur,
> It answers with a purr, purr, purr;
> And in its drooping half-shut eye,
> A dreamy pleasure we espy.

---

* There is something in the operation of shaving which, besides its painfulness, ought to make it repulsive to those who do not shave themselves—such as having the face bedaubed with lather and rubbed with a brush, which has done the same office for hundreds of chins. It is amusing to hear a knot of free and independent Englishmen roaring, "Britons never will be slaves;" most of whom will give their chins to be mown and their noses to be pulled by any common Barber, and pay him too for the pulling. Even when the party is a self-shaver, to say nothing of the waste of time, what a number of petty annoyances and exercises of temper does it involve! Notwithstanding the boasts of cold water shavers, depend upon it in rigorous weather most people prefer hot to cold water, which renders them slaves to their servants; next, razors, as we know from puff advertisements and our own experience, are the most uncertain of articles; then there is the state of the nerves, that even the strongest cannot always control, causing the unsteady hand to gash and hack the chin, or cover it with blood from the beheading of those pimply eruptions of which the razor has been ofttimes the originator.

And while the result of shaving is a mere negation, depriving us of a natural protection, and exposing us to disease, the other process, consume what time we will, is natural and instinctive, and attended with the satisfaction of adding the grace of neatness to nature's stamp of man's nobility.

III. *"That the ladies don't like it!"* This Professor Burdach and Dr. Elliotson, pronounce a foul libel.* Ladies by their very nature like every thing manly; and though from custom the Beard may at first sight have a strange look, they will soon be reconciled to it, and think, with Beatrice, that a man without, "is only fit to be their waiting gentlewoman."[†] I have already mentioned one instance of a queen despising her husband, because he was priest-ridden enough to shave; and here I present you with a second in this veritable portrait (shewing it) of a painter in the reign of George I, of the name of Liotard, who having returned from his travels in the East, with this fine flow of curling comeliness, was irresistible. He followed his fate, and married, but then, alas, unhappy wretch! took one day the whim to shave off his Eastern glory. Directly his wife saw him, the charm of that ideal which every true woman forms of her lover, was broken; for instead of a dignified manly countenance, her eyes fell

---

* Old Burton in his Anatomy of Melancholy adds his quaint testimony. "No sooner doth a young man see his sweetheart coming, than he smugs up himself, pulls up his cloak, ties his garter points, sets his band and cuffs, sticks his hair, *twires his Beard,*" &c.

D'Israeli also says, "when the fair sex were accustomed to behold their lovers with Beards, the sight of a shaved chin excited feelings of horror and aversion; as much indeed as in this less heroic age would a gallant whose luxuriant Beard should 'Stream like a meteor to the troubled air.' "

† The whole dialogue from whence this phrase is taken, is suggestive of the contempt with which the ladies of Elizabeth and James the 1st's time regarded a hairless chin. And there are numerous passages in our old Dramatists which might be quoted to the same effect, but that some of the allusions do not square with modern notions of delicacy.

upon a small pinched face, with nose celestial and mouth most animally terrestial,

> And such a little perking chin,
> To kiss it seemed almost a sin!

IV. *"That a Beard may be very comfortable in Winter but too hot in Summer!"* The better races of the sons of torrid Africa wear Beards, as did the ancient Numidians, and Tyro-African Carthaginians before them. The Arab in the arid parching desert cherishes his! Are we afraid of being warmer than these in an English Summer? Besides, as we have already shewn, the Beard is a non-conductor of heat as well as cold.*

Having now, ladies and gentlemen, offered proofs that the Beard is a natural feature of the male face, and designed by Providence for distinction, protection, and ornament, and shewn you historically, that while there was never any sufficient reason alleged for leaving it off, unless a heaven condemned superstition, or the capricious dictates of fops and profligates, afford to any sound mind reasonable motives of action, need I ask you not to oppose the efforts of those who, reverencing the Creator's laws as above the dictates of man, conceive themselves justified in returning to the more natural course. On our part we will, notwithstanding all that we have said, freely allow any one to continue the practice of

---

* It is scarcely conceivable what strange remarks have been made to me on the subject of the Beard. One party very gravely enquired whether I really thought that Adam had a Beard? Another was remonstrating with me on the first manifestations of my moustache; against whom I wickedly urged the argumentum ad feminam—you don't object to it in the military? when the daughter naively chimed in, "why you know, Sir, *it is natural to them!*" Two or three acute persons, one of them a lawyer, have objected, "but you have your hair cut!" To which I have replied, "yes! but I don't shave it off; and I trim my Beard instead of removing it. You also pare your nails; but you don't think of plucking them out, do you?"

shaving, who will be content with the same plea as a certain Duke de Brissac, who was often overheard uttering the following soliloquy while adjusting his razor to the proper angle:

> Timoleon de Cosse, God hath made thee a Gentleman, and the King hath made thee a Duke; it is right and fit, however, that thou shouldst have something to do, therefore thou shalt shave thyself!